The

Greenapolis

Seven

Volume 2

M W JOHNSON

This is a work of fiction. The characters and events in it are inventions of the author and do not depict any real persons or events. Any resemblance to actual people or incidents is entirely incidental.

The
Greenapolis
SEVEN

Stopping Sticky Fingers

By

M W JOHNSON

Text Copyright 2012 by M W Johnson

ISBN 1469934795

EAN-13 9781469934792

M W JOHNSON

Preface

Children of all ages from preschoolers to adolescents can be tempted to steal for different reasons. Adolescents know they are not supposed to steal, but might steal for the thrill of it or because their friends do. Some might believe they can get away with it. As they get more control over their lives, some adolescents steal as a way of rebelling.

M W JOHNSON

Stealing is wrong, and the best way to understand it is to examine your child's thinking. Kids who steal often feel entitled to what they are stealing, even though they or their parents cannot afford it. There is a fierce sense of competitiveness among teens and pre-teens these days regarding having the cool stuff, wearing the hip clothes, and sporting hot make-up or accessories. Many kids will resort to stealing as a response to this phenomenon. Sometimes kids even steal for the sense of excitement it gives them, or do it under some type of peer pressure. A big part of the problem is that our society's message is completely absent of a strongly objective morality. In most movies and songs today, the

M W JOHNSON

bad people do good things and the good people do bad things, and everybody looks the same. Therefore, kids justify what they are doing. It is not surprising when kids develop some ambivalent feelings about integrity, character and the difference between right and wrong.

School-age children usually know they are not supposed to take something without paying, but they might do so anyway because they lack enough self-control.

Adolescents sometimes take things they want without understanding that things cost money and that it is wrong to take something without paying for it. Other complex reasons can be factors. They might be angry or want attention. Their behavior may reflect stress at home, school, or with friends. Some may steal as a cry for help because of emotional or physical abuse they are enduring.

In other cases, children and adolescents steal because they cannot afford to pay for what they need or want, for example, they may steal to get name-brand items. In some cases, they may take things to support drug habits. Although they have learned that theft is wrong, older children or teenagers steal for various reasons. A youngster may steal to make things equal if a brother or sister seems to be favored with affection, praise, or extra gifts. Sometimes, a child may steal as a show of bravery to peers, or to give presents to family or friends. Adolescents may also steal out of a fear of dependency; they do not want to depend on anyone, so they take what they need.

Whatever the underlying cause, if stealing is becoming a habit with your youngster or teen, consider speaking with a doctor or therapist to get to the cause of the behavior. It is also important to routinely monitor your youngster's behavior, keep him or her away from situations in which stealing is a temptation, and establish reasonable consequences for stealing if it does occur.

Stealing is unacceptable in a school or classroom and the behavior requires zero tolerance as it infringes the right of pupils and staff to feel safe.

I truly empathize with what parents are up against these days. The concept of right and wrong has taken a real beating in our recent history. Therefore, when you tell kids it is wrong to steal, they have limited formal moral and ethical training to use as a reference point. There is too much excuse making for kids' behavior. Adults say, "It's only a stage he's going through." On the other hand, he has ADD. Alternatively, his father is an alcoholic. In addition, they keep making those excuses until the child is in serious trouble. Things like developmental stages or mental health diagnoses or family influences have to be dealt

M W JOHNSON

with. No matter what parents you have, no matter what mental health diagnosis, no matter what stage you are in, it is wrong to steal because it hurts others.

Adolescents steal for a reason and you need to uncover this to be able to take corrective action. Stealing is a common problem. You should view it like any other mistake your child makes. It is something that has to be corrected, but it is not more than that. If you handle it properly, you can correct this problem quickly and easily.

Chapter 1

A full week has gone by since the seven dealt with Henry Simpkins and his bullying ways. There is still an occasional report of Henry Simpkins throwing his weight around, although nothing too serious. There were not too many incidents to speak of other than a few items missing from around the sprawling middle school. There is also an occasional student or two exposing their special abilities for all to see.

Ajay searched frantically for his digital meal card. He repeatedly patted himself down. Top shirt pocket, front pant pockets, and then the rear pockets. He repeated the process several times. His hands were moving so fast he appeared to be putting flames out.

His eyes darting to the floor searching, head moving right to left searching for his meal card.

"Hurry up! We don't have all day," someone shouted from the rear.

"Young man you must scan your card. Please keep the lines moving," the attendant was growing impatient. His breathing started to increase ever so rapidly. He hung his head to the left while rolling his eyes to the top of his closely shaven head.

"I can't find it. I'm sure I placed it in my top pocket," Ajay exclaimed!

"Come on Ajay we are starving back here," Ajay could here the voice of Cody coming somewhere from the rear of the line.

"Here you are Ajay, your card is right here on the floor," yelled Dena.

Dena standing three places behind an annoyed Ajay hands him his meal card, he then passes it to the impatient attendant, who quickly scans the card before yelling "next" to Dena. "Thanks Dena, you're the greatest," Ajay sighed. He could not figure out how his card managed to end up at Dena's feet. Ajay was certain that he placed the card in his upper left pocket as it got closer and closer to breakfast.

The one thing Ajay was always ready for is a meal. Ajay could sense that something fishy was going on. This was the second time in as many days that his meal card decided to take a vacation. He was going to have to pay closer attention to it. Maybe I should tie a string on to it he wondered to himself.

The seven finally made it through the lunch line without any more delays. The friends sat together as they did at every breakfast and lunch. Ajay never said a word before consuming a hearty breakfast burger with a side of baked hash brown potatoes. Ju-long dined on a serving of cream of wheat with a grilled turkey bacon sandwich.

Everyone was excited about the breakfast meeting. Gabriela planned to discuss the latest string of events. They were all hoping for some new adventure. Each of the seven experienced some missing items in the last week.

Someone even managed to steal Aaminah's veil. She removed it to cleanse her face. She only looked down for a few seconds, only to find it missing when she raised her head again. Other than that, things were quiet the past week since the neutralizing of the bully, although there were some reports of other students and teachers at Greenapolis Middle School missing various personal items.

Ju-long, Ajay, and Cody quickly finishes their meal. Sharon, Aaminah, and Dena watches as Gabriela tosses her salad around with her fork, while barely eating the neat pile of toast and assortment of organic fruit.

"If you're not gonna eat that I will be glad to help you out," said a wide-eyed Ju-long.

Ju-long already had his bear-like claw moving in the direction of Gabriela's plate. Without looking up, she gladly slid the un-eaten salad in his direction. Ju-long without haste consumed the pile of fresh fruit without saying a word.

Gabriela waited another two full minutes before she spoke. You could always tell when Gabriela had something on her mind. There was always silence and a serious look on her face before she spoke. Gabriela looking up, made eye contact with each of them, and then she began to speak.

"Everyone did a nice job in neutralizing the bully. Now we have another situation to deal with. I am quite sure everyone is aware of the latest incidents that have occurred at school. There have been repeated instances of things missing," said Gabriela.

Dena, Cody, Ju-long, Sharon, and Aaminah all turned their heads in Ajay's direction. He was still running his hands along his body, as if he expected his card to disappear again.

"Each and every one of us has experienced it in the last week, things just don't walk away," she went on to say.

"Or do they?" asked Ajay.

"May I make a suggestion," Sharon barely pauses not allowing anyone to answer her question, while continuing to talk.

 "I think that everyone should pay real close attention to your personal property."

"Yea that's a good idea," Cody agreed.

"But I had my card right here in my top pocket, I am sure of it," Ajay interrupted.

Aaminah, speaking softly behind her veil simply said...

"I think we may have some sticky fingers running around in our school."

"Do you mean that someone is taking things that don't belong to them," asked Dena.

 "That's exactly what she means," answered Gabriela.

"What are we going to do about it?" Ajay wanted to know.

"I sure would love to find out what happened to my first meal card," Ajay displayed a sour look on his face.

 "Don't worry Ajay we will find out about your card, I promise you," responded Gabriela.

  M W JOHNSON

Gabriela was displaying the utmost look of confidence on her tanned face.

"Put it back," the voice shouted.

"I didn't do anything," yelled the second voice.

"You took my apple"

"Did not"

"Did to"

"Did not"

"What's going on over there?" asked Mr. Cousins.

"Someone took my apple"

"It was sitting right here," the shaky voice answered.

The sticky finger bandit was smiling and enjoying his work. He ran his fingers along the smooth skin of the apple tucked safely in his pocket. The Seven now turning their attention to the ruckus across the room, stared in awe. They exchanged glances at each other while having the same thought. There is someone with sticky fingers among us. "*We must stop sticky fingers.*"

Chapter 2

Gabriela, Ajay, Dena, Cody, Sharon, Ju-long, and Aminah sat quietly without uttering a word. Mr. Cousins, always circling the spacious dining area quickly quieted the ruckus, threatening whoever the culprit might have been with a stern warning.

"If and when I find out who took the apple, I am taking you straight to the Dean of Students," he quipped.

The students mostly giggled at the threat Mr. Cousins proclaimed. After only a week in school, the students all realized that Mr. Cousins is more bark than bite. He is not much to look at. Standing about five feet tall, weighing no more than one hundred and twenty pounds. Mr. Cousins is not much taller than most of the students attending Greenapolis Middle School.

No one seemed to take him serious, except maybe the apple-less Molly Pender. She sat there the entire time with big red glassy eyes, peering about while silently hoping that her apple would appear as mysteriously as it disappeared.

"I guess whoever or whatever it is must have quite an appetite," said an explaining Ajay.

"Yea, electronic meal cards, and apples to say the least," responded Dena.

"Maybe we can set a trap for whoever it is," Sharon suggested.

"That is a great idea," we definitely have a sticky finger bandit on the loose," said Ju-long

"Wait a minute, not so fast, we have to try and figure out who or what we are dealing with," insisted Gabriella.

"You mean we have to come up with a plan," Dena asked.

"Exactly," responded Aaminah.

"Between the seven of us we should be able to come up with some kind of way to corral this person who takes things without permission," Aaminah spoke while peering behind her silk veil.

"I think I know exactly who to consult, we must gather all the facts," Gabriela said with a smile. "We will deal with this in the same manner in which we dealt with Henry Simpkins the former bully. We will investigate and gather all the information we can before we do anything. After we have finished our research we will take the corrective action we need to deal with this sticky finger bandit."

Gabriela, spoke with her usual authority.

Gabriela was hoping her dear friend Sam would eventually make himself available, preferably sooner than later. She had no way of contacting him; however, he always seems to show up when she needed him the most. Like the time they were confronted with the bully. Sam always came to her rescue at just the right time, giving Gabriela all the information she and her friends needed to deal with whatever the situation is.

"Everyone pays attention to their belongings," Gabriela commanded.

"It is almost time to move on to the rest of our classes." Ajay clutched his digital board closer to his body, at the same time appearing fearful for his belongings.

"I don't want anyone else to loose one single item," Gabriela spoke with confidence.

"Its time to go to classes everyone," Cody spoke quickly before turning and walking away.

"I guess we will all meet up at lunch," said a soft-spoken Aaminah.

Ju-long turned his attention towards Sharon while asking her, "Are you ready to tackle some math my smart friend?"

"Do you mean, am I ready to help you today?" Sharon answered with a smile.

"Whatever," Ju-long responded jokingly.

The unmistakable sound resonated throughout the facility. It was time to move on. The seven began the journey to their respected classes.

 M W JOHNSON

Dena and Cody headed in the direction of sunshine alley. Aaminah and Ajay nodded in agreement while reluctantly starting in the direction of ancient history class.

"Time to head to go green class," reported Cody.

"Yea it's great to be able to learn how to protect and preserve our planet," said an excited Dena.

Dena with her American Indian heritage, felt very close to nature and the animals.

Gabriela slowly heads towards her language arts class, but not before reminding everyone about the up coming meeting at lunch.

"Everyone please be on time today. We have tons of work to do with little time to do it."

"She's right, I see more problems ahead. Things will get worse before they get better," said Dena.

"Are you breaking the rules, and using your gift of sight again?" kidded Cody.

"I suppose so, sometimes I can't help myself. Things just come to me," replied Dena.

 M W JOHNSON

Chapter 3

To Dena's surprise, she and Cody easily made it to Go Green Class without any incidents. The remainder of the students trickled into class. They managed to make it to their respective seats just as the infamous chime finished resonating throughout

Greenapolis Middle School. Everyone knew the rules. You have to be in your seat before the chime ends. There is little tolerance for tardiness at the Greenapolis Middle School. The classes started on time all the time. All the staff made sure that the popular middle school was operating at peak efficiency.

The teacher methodically went through the motions of accounting for the students that are present and the ones that are not. After hearing their respective names, Cody and Dena exchanged cheerful glances at each other. The students prepared their digital boards for today's lesson. Before class starts, each student receives a micro card to insert into his or her digital board for note taking.

     M W JOHNSON

The teacher then collects the cards after the lecture and grades them accordingly. Greenapolis Middle School is big on note taking. The staff is always judging students on how much information they absorb. Measuring comprehensiveness is one of the ways the staff keeps the students focused. The students receive grades immediately after each class.

Without any warning or introduction, Mr. Melloeasy began...

"Today's lesson is 10 easy ways to go green," he said with authority.

He went on to say that students needed to be smart energy consumers in order to succeed in the future. He also said that if our schools are going to do a good job of preparing the students for the challenges they will face in their lifetime then we must teach them how to manage the resources available to them. Mr. Melloeasy pauses for just a moment allowing the class to catch up to him. The only sound you could hear was the tapping of busy fingers across at least two dozen digital boards.

He took a deep breath before continuing. "How many of you are aware that just by turning off the faucet while brushing your teeth you can save up to two hundred gallons of water per month," he barely paused.
A few hands shot up in the air. Mr. Melloeasy ignored them while continuing with his lecture. "Here are some other things to consider," he blurted out.

Mr. Melloeasy said to turn off the lights when leaving a room, even if you are coming right back to the room. Take shorter showers. Use a water filter to purify tap water instead of drinking bottled water. Mr. Melloeasy explained to the students that bottled water is expensive and it creates large amounts of container waste. He said that using cold water to wash clothes saves on the cost of heating the water. Mr. Melloeasy stressed the importance of using both sides of the paper when printing or copying. He said that by doing this we could save many trees. One of the most interesting things Mr. Melloeasy shared with the class was to unplug unused electrical items.

Mr. Melloeasy informed the class that the chargers we use to charge our digital boards consume electricity even when our boards are free from them. He said that these are known as phantom loads, and that 25% of electricity consumed in our homes is because of things left plugged in. He advised the class to unplug the chargers until it is time to charge your board again. Mr. Melloeasy even gave the class a few tips to share with the parents. He informed the class to tell their parents that less fuel equals more money and better health. Mr. Melloeasy said to tell them to walk or bike to work instead of using the pod. This will save on fuel and parking cost while improving your cardiovascular health and reducing the risk of obesity.

Dena sat quiet as a church mouse. She was extremely excited to hear all the interesting and fun facts about the planet. She always felt very close to nature. All the things Mr. Melloeasy was telling the students made her want to do even more to preserve the earth.

Cody was already getting bored. While the other students struggled to keep up, he effortlessly typed away on his digital board. Thanks to his uncanny eye-hand coordination.

Chapter 4

Sharon along with Ju-long stared at the clock on the wall. The clock's emotionless face, displayed only the time. The second hand struggled to reach nine and then ten. Ju-long could hardly wait for the math session to end. Math was hardly his favorite subject.

He preferred to tinker with the insides of some computer or digital device. Even though Ju-long was ten times stronger than most teenagers were his age, his father taught him at an early age to suppress his abnormal strength. His father explained to him that using his brain would take him farther than using his brawn. He said that there would come a time when using his strength would be necessary. Ju-long remembers his father once telling him that he had to be good in math if he wanted to succeed in computers. That eventually everything comes back to numbers to some degree.

The jolt he felt to his chair startled him. It was Sharon using her foot to rattle him back to reality. His eyes meeting hers she mouthed the words...*pay attention.* Ju-long smiling and nodding his head in agreement tuned his eyes to the large transparent electronic smart board the teacher was using to explain the complicated steps of the mathematical procedure.

The numbers appearing and disappearing under the light touch of the instructors nimble fingers. Ju-long typed furiously. His momentary gazing caused him to slip behind in his note taking.

Sharon watched her friend struggle to catch up with the lesson. She of course had no problem figuring out what the instructor is trying to teach the class. Sharon simply loves the fact that she can just about solve any math problem there is. She was already way ahead of all the students in the class, and sometimes ahead of the teacher as well.

Sharon thought of the sticky finger bandit the seven discussed earlier in the day. She was hoping that Sam would communicate with Gabriela so that the seven could come up with a plan to rid the school of the situation. She thought about Henry Simpkins the school bully, and how the seven worked as a team to neutralize him.

Sharon, slightly annoyed by the shove she received from behind on her shoulder, turned around to see a teary-eyed Chance Needleblum.

"What is the matter Chance?" Sharon asked.

He spoke; his voice shaky, barely above a whisper.

"Have you seen my communicative device? It was right here on my desk," he moaned.

"No I have not seen it," Sharon responded, quickly surveying the space around her.

"My mother is going to kill me," said a visibly shaken Chance Needleblum.

Ju-long, sitting next to Chance, placed his oversized strong hand on the shoulders of the smaller Chance Needleblum.

"Don't worry my little friend, we will help you locate your communicative device," said a reassuring Ju-long. He looked about the room as if he was expecting to see the device.

     M W JOHNSON

Sharon's eyes met Ju-longs. The two friends had little doubt as to what they think happened to poor Chance Needleblum's communicative device. They were almost certain it had to be the sticky finger bandit. The commotion in the room caused Mrs. Melloeasy who is also the wife of the Go Green instructor Mr. Melloeasy to pause during the furious pace of the lesson.

"If I were you I would pay attention," she bellowed, casting her gaze in the direction of Sharon, Ju-long, and Chance.

Sharon raised her hand.

"What is it young lady? Mrs. Melloeasy asked.

"Chance Needleblum is missing his communicative device," Sharon answered.

"It was right there under his desk," Ju-long butted in.

"My mother is going to kill me," bellowed Chance Needleblum.

"Everyone will have to be scanned before leaving the room," said Mrs. Melloeasy.

"If it is here we will find it," she said.

"Now if the three of you do not mind and with your permission I will continue today's lesson," said a sarcastic Mrs. Melloeasy.

Chapter 5

The Students were already standing; crowding the doorway, the chime to move on to the next class still resonating in the background.

"I need everyone to form a straight line please," said a commanding Mrs. Melloeasy.

The students were anticipating the scanning promised to them by Mrs. Melloeasy, before they were able to leave the class. Ju-long, the biggest of the group jumped to the front of the line. Ju-long always took advantage at the opportunity to be the first at something. He liked to prove that he is brave and not afraid of any situation. Ju-long wanted everyone to be aware of the fact that he would never engage in such foolishness. He has never taken anything from someone else without his or her permission nor did he have any plans to. In all of his great wisdom, Ju-longs father taught him at an early age to respect the property of others. He said that it was wrong to steal. That there were other ways to obtain the things that someone wanted without stealing them.

One by one in steady fashion, Mrs. Melloeasy moved the handheld device from child to child. The tiny electronic device easily fit in the palm of her small hand. The device somehow transmitted tiny pictures of any non-organic materials located on the body to a larger display located at the front of the class. The device omitted an occasional beep causing the children to giggle, as she quickly moved from child to child, however it did not reveal the whereabouts of Chance Needleblum's property.

The entire incident took less than one full minute.

"Okay everyone, its time to move on to your next class," declared a somber sounding Mrs. Melloeasy.

She walked up to Chance Needleblum and said that she was sorry for his loss and that she would keep an eye out for his property. She informed him that she would file a missing item report. None of those words made him feel any better. The sticky finger bandit had struck again, Sharon thought to herself. Sharon moved into the direction of her dear friend.

"Ju-long, how could Chance's communicative device just disappear without a trace?" She asked.

"That's a good question. It's as if it just got up and walked away," responded a puzzled Ju-long.

"I saw your communicative device earlier in the class session it was right under your desk as you said it was," said Peter Poindexter.

Chance did not respond.

"Chance, was your device a weird looking blue color?" Jermaine asked.

"Yes it was, it is tiffany blue as my mother put it, with a silver streak down the middle," responded a semi-enthusiastic Chance Needleblum.

"That's funny; I saw it resting right here on the shelf by the door during the lesson," answered Jermaine.

"How can that be," asked Chance.

"Then where did it go?" Ju-long wondered aloud.

"That's a good question Ju-long, everyone was searched, and Mrs. Melloeasy did not find anything," Sharon said.

"Gabby's gonna love this," said a smiling Ju-long.

"I saw it also," said Molly Pinder.

"You did, where?" Responded a suddenly rejuvenated Chance.

"I didn't want to say anything earlier. I did not want you guys to think that I was nuts or something," her voice barely above a whisper.

"Well," Chance was growing impatient.

M W JOHNSON

"Give her a chance to speak," Ju-long demanded.

"Take your time Molly, don't be afraid," Sharon was trying to sound reassuring.

Molly could feel the ten or so sets of eyes that were bearing down on her.

"It's ok," Sharon urged.

Molly hesitated, but she started to speak.

"I first noticed it under his desk like Jermaine pointed out..."

"Go on, then what?" questioned Chance.

"The next time I looked that way, it was gone...I thought that maybe you moved it or something...then I caught a slight movement from the corner of my eye. I wasn't sure but I thought I saw your device move without any help. Every time I looked, the device was sitting under a different desk. The last place I saw it was on the shelf nearest the door just where Jermaine says he saw it."

Everyone except Chance, Sharon, and Ju-long burst into uncontrollable laughter.

"I knew that all of you would laugh at me. I know what I saw," said a teary-eyed Molly.

"Don't worry Molly we believe you," said Sharon.

M W JOHNSON

Chapter 6

Sharon and Ju-long could hardly wait to see Gabriela and the others. They could not wait to tell their friends the new twist to the sticky finger bandit caper. The two of them hurriedly made their way through the crowded hallways. Unfortunately, for them they were down to about three minutes before they had to be in the next class. The little scanning incident with Mrs. Melloeasy cost them about two precious minutes, two minutes they knew they needed to explain the new developments to their dear friends.

Ju-long grabbing Sharon by the hand wasted little time darting through the busy hallway.

"C'mon Sharon, lets go I will get us through this jumbled mess," he proclaimed.

Ju-long's strides were three times that of anyone else's therefore the two of them were moving three times as fast as the other students were.

 M W JOHNSON

"Woooo…slow down big guy, we don't want the hall monitor to give us a speeding ticket," Sharon said with a giggle.

"Don't worry Sharon, I can clearly see above everyone. I promise to slow down in the event the hall monitor surfaces."

Ju-long zigzagged effortlessly in and around the other students. They all seemed to be standing still. Sharon squeezed his hand tighter as they whizzed by the other students. Ju-long glancing over his shoulder smiling as Sharon opened and closed her eyes several times during the ordeal.

"Hey, slow down," someone shouted.

Finally, the two of them made it to sunshine alley, the main hallway in the Greenapolis

Middle School. All the other hallways intersect with sunshine alley. Ju-long turned the last corner barely coming to a screeching halt, almost pummeling into his five friends.

"Made it," said a sweaty and out of breath Ju-long.

Sharon did not say a word. She was trying to put her hair back together, the obvious result from her wild ride with Ju-long.

"What in the world is going on with you two?" Cody asked.

"You guys are not going to believe this," said Ju-long while trying to catch his breath.

"Believe what," asked Gabriela.

"Yea, we don't have a lot of time here," said Ajay.

    M W JOHNSON

"Lets hear it already," said an impatient Dena while glancing at the large wall clock. There are three minutes to go and counting until the next session. Aaminah waited patiently not saying a word.

"I think we should walk and talk," Gabriela said using her leader voice.

"You see Sharon and I were in Math class and Chance was crying," said an excited Ju-long.

"And?" said Ajay.

"Slow down and go ahead," demanded Gabriela.

"Well you see it seems as if perhaps the sticky finger bandit has struck again," Ju-long continued.

Ju-long looked to Sharon for help. She did not hesitate or disappoint. Jumping right in she gladly took over the conversation.

"Chance Needleblum asked me if I saw his communicative device. He said that he placed it underneath his desk, when he went to check on it there was nothing there," Sharon calmly said.

"Really?" asked a soft-spoken Aaminah.

"Yes, really, but get this, here comes the best part," responded Sharon.

Ju-long butted in before Sharon could finish.

"Do you guys remember Molly Pinder, The girl whose apple was stolen this morning at breakfast? Well she claims to have seen the device at different places at different times during the class session. Jermaine claims to have seen the device on the shelf nearest the door," Ju-long stated.

Before anyone could utter a word Ju-long continued to speak.

"She claims to have seen it move.... all by itself," Ju-long paused.

The others stopped walking looking at Ju-long as if he were crazy.

"What are you saying," Cody asked.

"What I'm saying is the device was there and then it was not, that's what I'm saying."

"I think the sticky finger bandit may have left us a clue," said Ajay.

"What kind of clue," Dena wanted to know.

"We are out of time now we will continue the discussion at lunch today, maybe Sam will surface and give us some advice," said Gabriela.

The Greenapolis Seven split into several groups making their way down the connecting hallways. All seven were intrigued with the latest developments and were extremely excited to get through the last class session before lunch.

     M W JOHNSON

Chapter 7

Gabriela sat unusually quietly in her seat. She normally would engage in any topic or discussion the teacher led. Her mind was far far away from the subject of mannerisms and etiquette. The class is a requirement at the school, meaning every student had to enroll in the class. Gabriela remembers how she argued with her mother about why she had to take such a class. Her mother said the class would teach girls how to behave like young women and boys how to behave like young men. The class Etiquette and Mannerisms encourages others to behave in a proper manner and to earn the respect of others.

Gabriela was thinking about the new developments surrounding the sticky finger bandit that surfaced today. With all the enchanted students, attending Greenapolis Middle School there could be some truth to the so-called walking communicative device.

She had to come up with a way to follow the minimal leads that the seven had to work with.

     M W JOHNSON

She thought hard and long about any abilities from any of the other students that could cause an item to move around unassisted.

She would have Cody, Aaminah, Dena, Ajay, Sharon and Ju-long go through their list of friends as well. There had to be a connection between the students and the missing items. They would also have to question their friends and classmates to see if they have any items missing. If so, they were to ask them if they noticed anything unusual. That alone would be a difficult question considering that the school itself is unusual along with the majority of the students.

Gabriela possessed the abilities to figure most things out on her own, although she grew accustomed to having her lifelong friend Sam advise her from time to time. She had no way of calling on Sam. He just somehow appeared, always on her left shoulder, always in a different form.

Sam told Gabriela that only she could see and hear him. Sometimes Sam appeared as a little furry animal. Other times Sam appeared in a humanoid form. Regardless of what form he took, it was never one, which she had seen before. Sam never took the same form twice. Yet his voice is always the same, soft, confident, and reassuring.

"Hello Gabby," said the soft voice.

Sam's reassuring voice quickly tuned her attention back to the present situation.

"Hello Sam, it sure is nice to hear your voice again," Gabriela replied.

"Did you think I would leave you alone to handle the sticky finger bandit?" Sam asked.

"Of course not, although you did take your time getting here," said a sarcastic Gabriela.

"Ok Sam why do you think this thing or person or whatever is stealing?"

"Well Gabby he or she could be stealing for a number of reasons," answered Sam.

Cody sitting two rolls over from his dear friend Gabriela smiled as he saw Gabriela nodding her head as if she were agreeing with someone or something. He was certain Gabriela was communicating with her elusive friend Sam.

Sam offered the following explanation to Gabriela. Very young children sometimes take things they want without understanding that things cost money and that it is wrong to take something without paying for it.

School-age kids usually know they are not supposed to take something without paying, but they might do so anyway because they lack enough self-control.

Preteens and teens are aware that they are not supposed to steal, but might steal for the thrill of it or because their friends do. Some might believe they can get away with it. As their parents give them more control over their lives, some teens steal as a way of rebelling.

     M W JOHNSON

There are other complex reasons that may be factors. Kids might be angry or want attention. Their behavior may reflect stress at home, school, or with friends. Some may steal as a cry for help because of emotional or physical abuse they are enduring.

In other cases, kids and teens steal because they cannot afford to pay for what they need or want for example, they may steal to get popular name-brand items.

Gabriela tried her hardest to digest all the important information Sam laid on her, before she asked her next question.

"What can my friends and I do about the sticky finger bandit," questioned Gabriela.

Stopping Sticky Fingers

"Well my dear Gabby, the first thing you can do is secure all of your items. What I mean is do not create an easy environment for the bandit to steal. Limit the opportunities. If I were you Gabby, I would inform my friends to keep an eye out for an unusual behavior by the other students."

"That will be hard to do in this place, everything and everyone is unusual here," Gabriela joked.

"Well Gabby, you are all loaded with knowledge now. Take the information I gave to you and share it with your friends. Together you can formulate a plan, and then put an end this sticky finger bandit character.

Chapter 8

Gabriela was all smiles marching down sunshine alley towards the soon to be crowded dining area. She could hardly wait to share all the wonderful information with her six best friends. She turned towards Cody, urging him forward.

"C'mon Cody we have plans to make."

"Ok, Gabriela I'm right here. You don't have to worry about me wasting time I'm starving," said a giddy Cody.

Gabriela waving both arms over her head motioned her hands towards Ju-long and Sharon who was approaching from her left. Not far behind them were Ajay, Aaminah, and Dena.

"Why are you so hyped?" Ju-long asked.

"I have an entire plethora of information to share with all of you," responded Gabriela

"I cannot wait to hear all about it," said Aaminah.

"Yea me too," echoed Ajay and Dena.

"Ok Cody, you find us a table while we hold a place for you in the line," ordered Gabriela.

"Will do captain," said a playful Cody.

Cody proudly took the front, leading the seven to the dining area. He was glad to know that Gabriela trusted and relied on him to find a table for the seven to eat plan and discuss.

"What is all the commotion up ahead?" Ajay asked.

There was a rather large crowd gathering near the entrance of the dining area. The students began to push and shove each other to get a closer look.

"Hey Ju-long, you are way up there towering over everyone, can you see what is going on?" asked Sharon.

"Funny, I'm not that tall silly girl," answered Ju-long.

"They seem to be pointing at something moving along the ground. I cannot see what they are pointing at," said Ju-long

"What is the problem up there? Clear the doorway," the hall monitor yelled loudly.

"Hang on everyone, I'm gonna try and work my way a little closer to the situation," said a confident Ju-long.

"Don't hurt anyone big boy," said a usually stoic Aaminah.

"Will do," responded Ju-long.

After a couple of long strides and a few shoves, Ju-long made his way to the front of the melee. He slowed wiping his eyes not

     M W JOHNSON

believing what they were telling him. Some of the students were yelling. Others were checking their eyes in dis-belief. A few more were pointing and laughing at what they thought they were seeing.

Ju- long began pushing his way closer and closer until his view was unobstructed. There it was clear as day. Just inside the doorway, a meal card, a pink communicative device, and a digital notebook. Ju-long thought he had seen everything, but this site was unbelievable. The three items were running around like squirrels. They had legs and arms but no head. Ju-long, asked himself how could that be? What could cause things that are not living to run around?

The hall monitor, following the blazing trail Ju-long cut through the crowd was peering over Ju-longs left shoulder. He too could not believe what was happening. Stepping around Ju-long the hall monitor walked towards the three items. The closer he got to the three items the more they ran around.
"Alright Alright, that's enough, he said, bending over and completely out of breath.

The sticky finger bandit grinning from ear to ear was enjoying his work. He smiled and laughed with the rest of the students. The items ran and stopped a few more times before resting under a nearby table. The monitor quickly picked the items up before they could take off running again. The sticky

  M W JOHNSON

finger bandit settled in among the crowd unnoticed.

Gabriela, Cody, Aaminah, Dena, Sharon, and Ajay all made their way to Ju-longs side.

"Wow, now that was a show," said an excited Dena.

"You said a mouthful Dena," Ajay replied.

"Okay gang, Cody found us a table over there," said a pointing Gabriela.

"Let's get our food, eat, and formulate a plan to foil the sticky finger bandit before he strikes again," said Gabriela.

"That sounds like the best idea you've come up with today," mocked Ju-long.

Chapter 9

The noon lunch meeting consisted of Gabriela, Ju-long, Ajay, Dena, Aaminah, Cody, and Sharon, with the exception of Molly Pinder. Molly had felt a sense of closeness and support since the earlier episode in math class. She appreciated the fact that Sharon and Ju-long did not make fun of her when she told them about the movements of Chance Needleblum's communicative device.

Usually the other students made fun of her when she said things. They teased her and called her silly among other names. The Greenapolis Seven made her feel welcomed and comfortable whenever she came around them. She could be herself without being ridiculed and chastised. She did not even have to talk if she did not want to.

The seven made it through the lunch line without any further incidents. Ajay reaching carefully into his pocket was relieved to feel the composite plastic card exactly where he put it. After the latest developments, Ajay was certain he had been an earlier victim of the sticky finger bandit.

Ju-long as usual is the first to finish his meal, followed by Ajay. The remainder of the seven finished their meal while Ju-long waited to devour whatever the others did not eat. After several minutes of what seemed like much longer Ju-long using his large hands as a shovel went around the table scooping up the remains.

"I think we all have some idea of what we are up against," Gabriela said.

"I'm not quite sure what we are up against," responded Ajay.

"Whatever it is it's something that I have never seen before," quipped Cody.

"And neither have I," Dena agreed.

"Well what or whoever it is has to be stopped, they are definitely getting out of hand," Aaminah said.

"What I meant was that this is entirely different from the bullying that Henry Simpkins was doing," said Gabriela.

"What do you have in mind for this whatever," asked Ju-long.

"Yea, Gabriela I saw you talking to your friend Sam in class earlier. What did he have to say?" Cody asked.

Gabriela recalling every single detail of her conversation with Sam talked for the full ten minutes remaining in the lunch period. Ju-long, Sharon, Cody, Dena, Ajay, and Aaminah listened without interrupting. She informed the group of every single piece of information Sam gave her. She talked about the why, the who, and some of the remedies concerning people who take things without the permission of others. Most importantly, Gabriela stressed the importance of putting an end to the sticky finger bandit and restoring order to the Greenapolis Middle School.

"Now that we know a little of what is going on with the sticky finger bandit, what are we going to do next," asked Aaminah in her soft voice. She advised the others that many items belonging to other students have been missing from locker rooms, for example, watches, expensive tennis shoes, coats, hats, backpacks,

       M W JOHNSON

and money. Gabriela went on to say that, Rubarb Rollins was the student taking these items. A student saw him walking around the school wearing many of the missing items; another student in the gym class witnessed Rubarb's method of thief.

She said that Rubarb could make inanimate objects come to life, and then he could control their movements.

"So that's why all the missing items seemed to walk away," said Ju-long.

"How brilliant of you to notice Ju-long," Dena said jokingly.

"Here's what we are going to do next," said Gabriela.

The remaining six leaned in and listened carefully as Gabriela outline the plan she had to put an end to the sticky finger bandit. It's going to take the efforts of all seven of us she explained to them.

"Everyone must keep their eyes open and if we follow the plan to the letter this caper should be over by the end of the day," said a reassuring Gabriela.

"That's a great idea Gabriela, we will use our talents and skills collectively to corral this bandit," Sharon agreed.

"Ok everyone if there are not any questions lets move along before we are late to class."

"I have a question," said Ajay.

 M W JOHNSON

"Hurry the chime for the next class has already resonated," Sharon added.

"What if the sticky finger bandit strikes again before we meet again at recess?" questioned Ajay.

"Just keep your fingers crossed that the bandit goes along with our plan," Gabriela answered.

Chapter 10

Rubarb Rollins wasted little time displaying his unusual talent. He saw many strange talents displayed among the students during his stay at Greenapolis Middle School; however, he did not run into anyone who could do the things he could. There are a few students with some type of kinetic abilities, including Ajay. They could move items around a little or transport a thing or two; however, no one could turn inanimate objects to life and control them like Rubarb Rollins.

Rubarb wanted to take as many things as possible back to his home school. He was part of an experiment between Greenapolis and Bonton Middle School. The two schools agreed to exchange students for a limited two-week period.

The seven friends made their way down sunshine alley, the main hallway connecting all the other hallways to the remainder of the school. You had to walk down sunshine alley to get to the majority of the school.

Dena could not help but notice the horrible weather outside. She looked through the clear glass tube at the torrential rain coming down in heaps. Using her gift of sight, it did not take her long to realize the rain would not end anytime soon and that recess would have to be inside today. The plan Gabriela came up with should still work inside she thought.

She thought about her role in Gabriela's plan. The seven friends would have to break the rules at Greenapolis and rely on their special abilities to corral Rubarb Rollins. Prior to admission, the students along with their parents agreed not to use their special abilities to their advantage while at school.

     M W JOHNSON

Dena was supposed to use her gift of sight to see whether Rubarb would take the items the seven would lay out for him. Unfortunately, Dena has to be in the presence of the person that she is trying to read. That meant she could not tell the others anything until she was in the presence of Rubarb while at recess.

The resonating chime startled Aaminah. She went over Gabriela's plan repeatedly in her sharp mind. Gabriela's plan was flawless. Aaminah is more intelligent than anyone in Greenapolis is. She possesses an I.Q of 175. She reasoned to herself that the plan would succeed.

It was time for recess, time to corral the sticky finger bandit. Gabriela, Ju-long, Ajay,

Cody, Sharon, and Aaminah went over their roles for Gabriela's plan while heading for the massive indoor recess facility.

The seven students meant just outside the double doors to the main entrance. Gabriela went over the plan with everyone to be sure that everyone knew what to do and that everyone is on the same page.

"Now, let us remember we will not accuse Rubarb of stealing anything beforehand, we will set the bait for him, catch him, and then we will approach him," reminded Gabriela. "Remember he is still a person with feelings and emotions, we must show compassion towards him," preached Gabriela.

One of Gabriela's major strengths or weakness depending on how you look at it is her overwhelming compassion for others. She is always willing to forgive.

"Okay, why don't we just give him a group hug after he robs us blind and we bust him," said a sarcastic Cody.

One by one, Gabriela carefully listened to the roles of each of the remaining six. After reassuring herself, that everyone knew his or her part in the plan the seven friends one at a time entered the spacious recess area.

Heading towards the private changing areas or PCA's, the boys went to the left and the girls went to the right. Ajay immediately spotted

Rubarb Rollins walking about ten feet in front of them.

"There he is up ahead," Ajay said while pointing in the direction of Rubarb.

"Lets catch up to him," said Ju-long quickening his pace.

"Here we go," said an excited Cody.

The three friends quickly closed the gap between them and the unsuspecting Rubarb. An unsuspecting Rubarb continued to walk towards the PCA's. Ju-long immediately put the plan into place. He made sure that his voice was loud and clear before he spoke.

"Hey guys my parents gave me money this morning before they left for work. Would you

M W JOHNSON

two like to go to the mall with me after school today?"

"Sure, ok," echoed Cody and Ajay.

Rubarb Rollins slowed his pace, while listening intently to the conversation of the three friends.

"My parents asked me to be careful and not to lose my money; I thought I would keep it in my backpack and store it in my locker," Ju-long said loudly.

"That's a good idea, I will do the same with my money, Cody agreed.

Gabriela, Sharon, Aaminah, and Dena changed into their recess gear while waiting near the volleyball nets for Ju-long, Ajay, and Cody to emerge from the changing area.

"How do you think they are doing in there Gabriela," asked Sharon.

"Oh they are doing just fine," Dena said with a wink.

Ju-long, Ajay, and Cody quickly changed into their recess attire, totally ignoring Rubarb. They pretended to leave the area and headed toward the doors to the recess area. Instead, the trio doubled around the long columns of lockers. Rubarb did not waist anytime before he went to work.

The trio observing Rubarb was amazed at what they saw. The combination lock on Ju-longs locker sprouted arms and began turning the dials to unlock itself. The lock jumped to the ground and the door to the locker flung open. Next, Ju-longs money, coins, and bills alike lined up single file heading towards Rubarb's PCA.

"Now that is cool," said a grinning Ajay.

"Shhhh, quiet," Ju-long ordered.

After two minutes had passed, all of Ju-longs money marched like small soldiers into Rubarbs locker. Ju-long had witnessed enough. Standing up he shouted in Rubarbs direction.

"Hey sticky fingers, that's my money," shouted an angry Ju-long.

Startled, Rubarb tried to flee the area. He did not get far. Ajay using his kinetic abilities untied Rubarb's laces, causing him to stumble. Ju-long pouncing on him easily controlled him with his large powerful hands.

"Oh no you don't sticky fingers, you are coming with us. We have some people that want to talk to you," explained Cody.

The three friends surrounding Rubarb escorted him to a waiting Gabriela, Sharon, Dena, and Aaminah.

"Here he is, we caught him red-handed," Ajay said.

As Usual, Gabriela is the first to speak; it is not ok to take property from others without their permission she told Rubarb. We will not allow you to continue to take things at Greenapolis Middle School. You have until the end of the day tomorrow to return all the items from your locker to the rightful owners.

     M W JOHNSON

If not, we will report you to the Dean of Students.

Now it was Sharon's turn, to use her power of persuasion to convince him never to steal again. Her eyes locked with his eyes, after two more minutes of talking Rubarb promised to return all the missing items. He said that he did not intend to harm anyone with his actions and that he was sorry. Rubarb swore never to take another thing from anyone without his or her permission.

About The Author

Dr. Michael W. Johnson is a writer, speaker, and author. He is also a former middle school reading and math teacher. Michael was born in Newport News, Virginia. He has spent over twenty years of his life teaching, tutoring, mentoring, and coaching hundreds of adolescents. When he is not writing, speaking,

or spending time with his family he likes to
read, cook, and mentor adolescents. For more
information on M W Johnson, please feel free
to visit his website at
mwjohnsonphd.books.officelive.com

www.ingramcontent.com/pod-product-compliance
Lightning Source LLC
Chambersburg PA
CBHW071456030726

47593CB00003B/1029